QUIET
MARKETING

A calm, minimal approach to
business and online visibility for
highly sensitive solopreneurs

Danielle Gardner

Quiet Marketing / Danielle Gardner (1st ed.)

ISBN (hardcover) 978-0-6453138-0-2

Contents

Dedication

This book is dedicated to all the highly sensitive
solopreneurs of the world who are seeking a way
to be in the marketplace that feels good
to their heart and soul.

Disclaimer

The ideas offered in this book have made a real difference to my business, but they may not have the same outcome for you. I recommend you take what resonates and feels expansive, experiment with those things, and leave the rest.

Introduction

Quiet marketing is not about playing small, being shy or being invisible in the marketplace.

It's about inspiring positive change in the world through your message.

It's about communicating your values, rejecting marketing trickery and 'fear of missing out' (FOMO) tactics.

It's about having a high level of integrity when you communicate to the marketplace.

And it's about prioritising your wellbeing and trusting yourself, even when your ideas are contrary to what everyone else is saying and doing.

What most of us have been taught to do is 'loud marketing'.

We've been taught we need to keep hustling, posting, boasting, and engaging so we can stay ever visible and avoid slipping through the internet.

But these marketing habits keep us energetically logged-on all the time and disconnected from the natural world.

They keep us reaching for our screens and consuming time that was intended for quiet moments of contemplation and rest.

The challenge with being a highly sensitive solopreneur is that we don't have the bandwidth for the level of online engagement that conventional marketing demands.

And when we try to make ourselves do these high-engagement strategies, we end up physically, mentally, and spiritually depleted.

What we crave more than anything is less time online and more time in the non-digital world. But we often ignore these desires because we believe that being visible everywhere, all the time, is the only way to be successful.

The inevitable outcome of conventional business and marketing advice is that we second-guess ourselves, our ideas, and our visions for how we really desire to be in business.

The quiet marketing approach aims to undo all this and lead you to a place where you trust and act on your ideas, you prioritise your wellbeing, and where your way of doing business and marketing feels like art.

Quiet marketing begins with quieting the outside world so you can return to your centre and the essence of who you are.

From this place, you can connect with your own divine spark, your own 'you-ness', your own way of communicating to the marketplace, and your unique way of delivering your offerings.

It's a slower, gentler, more minimal approach to business that flies directly in the face of consumerism, capitalism, and many of the widespread messages that we are presented with every day, telling us to be more, do more, and have more as quickly as possible.

If conventional business and marketing advice has not landed in your heart and soul very well, then this book is for you.

Have your journal handy so you can note down your thoughts and ideas as you go.

Re-imagining marketing

Imagine going about your marketing activities in a quiet, relaxed, minimal way where you feel like you are sharing important messages that can help people right now, and where you don't feel like you need to shout louder and be visible everywhere all the time to be noticed by your ideal clients.

How does that feel in your body?

The beautiful thing about being visible in this way is that you draw towards you like-minded people who don't just want your tips or strategies, they actually want to be associated with you because of who you are and how you think.

Welcome to the world of quiet marketing.

My journey

I've not always been a quiet marketer.

When I was taught to start my marketing copy with a list of pain point questions, I didn't question it.

When I was taught to build my list quickly through freebies, I didn't question it.

When I was taught I needed to be visible all the time on several different platforms and Facebook Groups, I didn't question it.

And when I was taught to discount and stack on bonuses in order to tip people over to 'buy now', I didn't question that either.

But then I started to question everything.

The catalyst for this turning point was when I decided to survey my audience about why they hop from one online training to another without implementing or completing the one prior.

The feedback I received was eye opening.

I could see so clearly how discounting strategies, fast action bonuses, countdown timers, and the promise of quick success kept people jumping from one bright shiny thing to the next, while making no significant change to their business.

I could see how these strategies we've all been taught are great for sales, but bad for people — and I could no longer be part of this way of being in business.

The following chapters chronicle the epiphanies and paradigm shifts that led me to developing a quiet, confident, and impactful approach to online visibility.

Enjoy!

1

Create your own definition of success

When you embarked on your self-employment journey, you probably felt like an exciting new chapter of your life had opened.

You imagined the possibilities, felt good about contributing to positive change in the world through your work, and looked forward to more time, freedom, and flexibility.

But then somewhere, somehow, that excitement turned into overwhelm, and you found yourself spending more and more time online.

That was my journey as well.

I had been striving for 'success', and yet I'd never actually articulated what success meant to me.

It was a huge lightbulb moment when I realised that I had unconsciously adopted a vision of success that was not congruent with who I am.

And as a result, I was rushing myself along, making myself do strategies that didn't feel good, and chasing metrics that were meaningful to others, but not me.

So, I opened up a new Google Document and reflected on the things that actually make me feel successful.

I knew it was important to come up with a definition that would allow me to feel successful every day, as opposed to 'someday' in the future.

The definition I typed onto the page was very simple, practical and grounding, and helped me to tune out other people's ideas of success and focus on what makes me feel good.

I revisit this definition a couple of times a year to see if it needs any tweaking.

Right now, this is what success means to me:

To have mental and physical space, be organised, do my art, share meaningful messages, have three days off per week, enjoy daily walks in nature, and make business decisions that are good for my mental and emotional wellbeing.

Notice how this definition is not dependent on anyone else but me?

For example, instead of saying something like, "To impact millions of people," which would make my success dependent on others, I focus simply on 'sharing meaningful messages'.

Have you written down your own definition of success?

If not, why not take a moment to do that now before continuing on with this book.

2

Practice tunnel vision

Many business teachings encourage us to keep an eye on what our industry peers are saying, doing, and offering. I believe this practice is harmful. Let me explain why.

Have you ever found yourself feeling pressured to be more visible on social media, do marketing in a certain way, or have certain kinds of offerings?

That probably happened because you kept seeing content pop up in your newsfeed or inbox from your industry peers.

And in seeing them do 'all the things', you quietly thought to yourself, "I should be doing more," even though you were already spreading yourself too thin.

Of course, you do need to have a way for people to discover you, but it doesn't need to look like others'.

What if you could sell your offerings without doing the predictable marketing things like 'going Live' all the time, doing free webinars, running 5-day challenges, or free discovery calls?

Somewhere within you, there is a 'uniquely you' way of making your offerings known, but you'll probably never discover that while you keep looking at what everyone else is doing.

Another way peer distraction creates harm is when you see someone talking about the exact topic you were planning to share about.

This can slide you into discouragement and feeling like you don't have a unique voice or message to share.

And yet, if you never saw what they shared, you'd still feel excited and empowered to say what you felt moved to say — true?

The remedy for these situations and staying in the integrity of your message and mission is what I call 'practicing tunnel vision'.

Practicing tunnel vision is about doing whatever is necessary to close yourself off from seeing other people's content, messages, and offerings.

For example, you probably need to unfollow, mute, filter emails or unsubscribe from peer content to avoid swinging off your centre and bursting your creative bubble.

I have done this myself, and it is so freeing!

These days I hardly ever see content from coaches doing similar work to me, and this simple practice is one of the things that contributes to my having a calm nervous system.

Take a moment now to consider what you can do to minimise peer distraction, and whose content you might need to remove from your view.

3

Minimise digital distraction

It is alarming how normalised digital distraction has become, and I believe this is at the heart of why so many of us feel scattered, disorganized, and confused about our priorities.

Push notifications from our phones and computers disturb our peace and productivity in a profound way.

We lose our train of thought, miss important instructions, leave things half done, fall down rabbit holes, and feed our addiction to being 'on' all the time.

Our devices are usually configured from the get-go to have notifications popping and pinging up on our screens, compelling us to click on them and take us away from whatever we were focused on.

As a highly sensitive, highly aware person, please do yourself a favour and switch off your notifications.

This might be tricky to work out for some devices, but it's worth finding out how to do it for the sake of your own sanity and for minimising your screen time.

But push notifications are not the only issue here.

Equally distracting is having multiple tabs open in your browser.

You may have turned off your notifications, but you'll still see when there is new email and social media activity if you have those tabs open in the background.

It's especially important to close background tabs when you are working on something that requires stillness and focus, such as business development projects, content creation, and bookkeeping.

The world can wait.

You don't need to respond to everything in the moment, and when you try, you are bound to miss important details and instructions, which means you'll need to go back and redo things.

Allowing notifications to direct your day and behaviours is the opposite to living an intentional life.

Instead, schedule a regular time each day where you can properly attend to your notifications and emails. I have a standing appointment with myself each day for this purpose.

While going about my day and retrieving information from my inbox, I do see when I have new emails, but because I have a set time for responding, I don't feel compelled to jump in and reply straight away, and this brings me so much calm.

What helps me honour this placeholder in my daily schedule is marrying it up with a virtual co-working session on the Focusmate.com platform, which I recommend you test drive for yourself. It's free to join.

Before moving on, jot down some thoughts on ways you can reduce digital distraction.

✽✽✽ 4 ✽✽✽

Give yourself
breathing space

For me, creating space to breathe in business started off as a nice philosophical idea for my Speedy Gonzalez nature.

Now it's one of my most important business practices, because the more space I give my ideas, responses, projects, and goals — the more pleasurable my work life becomes.

Here are some examples of how you can give yourself breathing space in business:

Be generous with your scheduling.

- Allow more time than you need for client and personal appointments.

- Give yourself space to actually get up from your desk in between sessions, as opposed to using those gaps to check emails.

- Instead of trying to squeeze clients into your already full week, get comfortable offering a date and time a few weeks down the track.

Make room to respond.

- Often our knee-jerk reaction to a trigger-ing email or comment is to respond straight away. The slow response, however, is always the more considered, more clear, and more compassionate one.

- My rule of thumb is to allow 24-hours before responding if I have felt triggered. You might like to try this too.

Give ideas time to incubate, develop, and mature, instead of releasing them to the marketplace prematurely.

- Your creations will increase in power and impact when they are wisely held, protected, and allowed to mature.

- I have found such value in this practice, and as a result my offerings have become more refined, aligned, and are more readily taken up.

Aim slower.

- It's the pace at which we expect things to happen in our business that causes most of our stress and anxiety. The paradox is that when we slow down and become more mindful with our actions and energy, we actually speed up our progress.

Have an alternative source of income.

- When we know that our financial needs are being met as we build or take time off from our business, we feel a luxurious inner spaciousness.

23

- Examples of alternative sources of income include part-time work for those in the building stage of their business, or passive income products for those more established.

Do any of the above examples speak to you?

Write down any action you feel inspired to take in order to give yourself more breathing space.

❧ 5 ❧

Follow your
Human Design strategy

Many of the highly praised business and marketing strategies work amazingly well for some people, and yet for a large majority of us, we can't get them to work very well at all.

And the more we hustle and strive with these strategies, the worse we feel energetically and emotionally.

Human Design teaches that the same advice is not correct for everybody because we are all designed differently, and each of us has a certain way of being in the world (our 'strategy') that leads to more effortless success.

What is Human Design?

Human Design is a holistic self-knowledge system combining astrology, the I Ching, Kabbalah, and Vedic philosophy.

The founder, Ra Uru Hu, received this knowledge in 1987 on the island of Ibiza, and for the next 25 years, dedicated himself to developing this profound and comprehensive system.

The system uses your date, time, and location of birth to calculate your BodyGraph chart, a blueprint for how you operate and interact with the world.

The information presented in the BodyGraph chart can be overwhelming, so if you are new to Human Design I recommend focusing on your:

1. Type

2. Strategy

3. Inner Authority

4. Profile Numbers

When I discovered my own Human Design, it was a real eye opener because I could see how I had been working in opposition to it, and therefore making it difficult to reach my business goals.

For example, my 'Strategy' for success is to 'respond' and yet I had spent my business life 'initiating' everything, which is why it took so much effort to gather interest in my offerings.

I also realised I'd been ignoring my 'Inner Authority' (my inner GPS), which had resulted in a series of regrettable decisions about how I work and whom I work with.

And after studying my 'Profile Numbers' I realised that my approach to marketing and desire to reach cold audiences was counterproductive to my design.

The changes I made as a result of these insights ushered in a new era of ease in terms of business offerings and sales, which is why I recommend you learn about your own Human Design if you have not done so already.

Your first step is to get your free Human Design Chart by going to: www.jovianarchive.com/get_your_chart.

Once you have your BodyGraph chart, start learning about your: Type, Strategy, Inner Authority, and Profile Numbers via the Jovian Archive website, YouTube, and the resources listed at danigardner.com/book-resources.

6

Reduce inputs to allow for outputs

Chronic content consumption has become the modus operandi for many online solopreneurs like us. I would even go as far as to say it has become an addiction.

This addiction is characterised by a weekly schedule of 'inputs' such as: attending free webinars, participating in 5-day challenges, and enrolling in yet another course or group program that we don't really need — which leaves little room for our own creations (i.e. outputs).

Outputs are activities that actually make a difference in terms of impact and income, and include things like: creating content that we can be discovered by, systemising and automating our operations, nurturing our networks, and developing leveraged offerings.

Here are some suggestions on how you can break the vicious cycle of chronic inputs so you can have the time and space to follow through with your own creations:

1. Practice tunnel vision, as discussed in Chapter 2. Unsubscribe, unfollow, mute. Do whatever is necessary to minimise temptation. You can't be distracted by bright shiny things that don't cross your path!

2. Identify an output/project/creation that you can channel your energy into each month or quarter, and see it through to completion.

3. Support yourself to follow through by having some kind of accountability measure, such as an accountability buddy/mentor/group, or by using the virtual coworking platform Focusmate mentioned earlier.

Which of these suggestions could you take action on right now?

7

Play the whole tape through

This is advice I received from one of my earliest business mentors, Gina DeVee, and boy did it stick to me like glue.

Way too often, I was not thinking beyond my initial excitement for an idea, opportunity, or thing I wanted to sign up for. And as a result, I'd end up exhausted from overextending myself.

Playing the whole tape through has helped me slow down for a minute, consider consequences, listen to my body, and from this place, make better decisions.

Here are some questions I like to ask as I play the whole tape through:

- Where will this fit in my weekly schedule?

- How much of my free time will this encroach on?

- What am I willing to give up in order to fit this thing in?

- Do I truly need this, or have I just been swooped up in a sassy marketing machine?

- Do I actually need more curriculum, or is it that I need a form of accountability/support to implement what I've already learnt?

- Is this what I really want, or am I just following what others are doing?

This simple idea of 'playing the whole tape through' has changed me from being someone who scurried around, jumping on every opportunity that crossed my path, to being highly discerning and quietly confident about my own way of doing things.

8

You don't need to make yourself accessible

Current-day marketing advice emphasises the use of Direct Messaging to communicate with and source clients.

However, play the whole tape through with this approach and you'll soon see that DM marketing requires more screen time, and probably makes you more accessible than you really want to be.

Please know that you absolutely do not need to make yourself accessible via DMs, social media comments or email in order to create a financially sustainable business.

Nor is it your 'duty' to be easily accessible to audience members or clients if you don't want to be.

When I evaluated my own use of DMs, I found there was no real value or benefit to being contactable through this medium to people I didn't already know.

For example, I'd often receive questions via direct message that could have easily been answered simply by clicking through to my website.

Being accessible via direct messaging ultimately gave me more unnecessary work, which is why I ended up changing my social media settings to limit who could reach out to me privately.

And what I've found since is that if someone is 'truly' interested in what I offer, they will go to my website and proactively find what they are looking for.

The other benefit of adjusting my messenger settings is that replies to my content end up in the comments with the other responses (where they belong), rather than a private message.

This tendency to make ourselves overly accessible extends into our client work as well.

We may adopt practices such as offering support in between sessions, simply because that's what we see others doing.

Of course, there may be legitimate reasons why support in between sessions needs to be offered. My point is to play the whole tape through and don't offer something that does not truly feel aligned for you.

You might wonder if being less accessible will have a negative impact on your business. In my case it hasn't, and I've only had positive feedback about it.

For some clients, the fact that I didn't make myself easily accessible inspired them to work with me because this is what they want for themselves.

Take a moment to contemplate where you are making yourself more accessible than you really want to be.

9

Trust your ideas, especially when they differ from what everyone else is doing

When I look back on the business and marketing education I've received, sadly, much of it left me second-guessing myself, my own ideas, and my authenticity.

Perhaps you can relate.

Obviously not all of our own cooked-up ideas are guaranteed to be effective; the point I want to make is that after all the indoctrination we've received, we can be very hesitant to even experiment and try them out.

Especially when we've hustled and strived to get some traction in our business. We fear losing momentum if we go 'off script' and do anything that's not part of the prescribed online marketing formula.

That standard formula looks something like this:

- Daily social media posting, commenting, and engaging

- Email opt-in (aka: lead magnet, freebie)

- Weekly newsletter

- Email sequence

- Free webinar/5-day challenge

- Early bird pricing/bonuses/countdown timer

- Money-back guarantee

My own business journey has seen me question every step of this formula.

Throughout this journey I kept asking myself...

"If I were to be really Dani, how would I do this?"

Then, little by little, I went rogue and replaced the standard formula with my own way of doing things.

The result?

I've never been more happy, financially success-ful, or felt more self expressed.

Was it easy to carve out a different path?

I didn't think it would be.

I thought I'd see a dip in income, but I was willing to take that risk for the sake of my inner compass and integrity.

However, my income didn't dip.

In fact, it has grown slowly and steadily since making these changes.

So, what does my rogue approach to marketing look like?

Below you'll see an overview of that, but first I want to emphasise:

a. I don't recommend you follow exactly what I am doing; I recommend you trust yourself and your ideas.

b. The way I go about things is not set in stone; it's fluid and evolves with time and my own preferences.

My current way of letting the marketplace know I exist:

- I prioritise written content such as blogs and YouTube videos where I share my knowledge and point of view. This is my art.

- Most people discover my content as a result of intentional Google searches on various topics. I don't have any sophisticated SEO strategy; I just have awareness of what my audience goes looking for, and I name my articles in a practical way, which makes it easy for search engines to find.

- After people discover me, they explore my other content pieces and start to get a good sense of who I am. This is when they decide they want to work with me (or not).

- I use social media ad campaigns to distribute my content to people who are already aware of me (aka my 'warm' audience).

- Currently I enjoy sharing my message on Instagram when I am inspired to. This is a form of self expression for me, not something I rely on for new business.

- In terms of list building, I used to have an option on my website to subscribe to my newsletter. Now it is only clients and students who have that option, and since making this change, I've had an increase in course sales.

- My group and 1:1 mentoring offerings are typically filled with my course students.

This way of being in business is working really nicely for me right now, but what about you?

If you were to be really 'you', how would you be in business?

Is there something I have shared that sparks interest for you?

Make a few notes on that now.

And remember, give yourself permission to experiment, break the rules and do what feels right for you.

>>> 10 <<<

Do less things better

What kept me spinning my wheels and not getting any lift-off in the first few years of business was that I was spreading myself too thin.

Then, when I stumbled upon the notion of doing less things, and doing them very well, this really struck a chord with me, and I started to change my approach.

- Instead of trying to be visible in multiple places at once, I pared back to one main social media platform, and having an active presence in just one Facebook Group*. As a

---

* I no longer have a presence in FB Groups for marketing purposes.

43

result, my impact was much greater and my sales increased.

- Instead of trying to work on several creations at once and not bringing any to completion, I zeroed in on one of them (which was a group offering), and four weeks later I launched my first group program. Then I moved on to the next creation.

- Instead of giving myself a dozen things to do in a week, or a day, I gave myself just a couple of things. And when I completed those things quicker than expected, I enjoyed the spaciousness of finishing early — rather than trying to cram a few more things onto my plate.

- I also pared back on the amount of content for my online classes to allow more time for discussion and integration, and this meant participants didn't go away feeling firehosed.

Being able to do less things better does require some mental reconditioning, because we tend to believe that success is a result of doing more.

But is that really true?

Doing more usually leads to complexity and stress.

To do less things better is to simplify.

Simplicity helps us exhale, relax, and accomplish more.

Which areas of your business and marketing could you be more effective in by doing less things better?

❯❯❯ 11 ❮❮❮

Look for the wisdom
in irritation

I've found that when there is irritation in my business, there is wisdom waiting to be uncovered.

Previously when I noticed a rising irritation with a client, audience member, peer, etc., I used to try and 'positive self talk' myself out of that feeling.

My inner voice would say something like, "You're better than this, you can rise above it."

But now I know it's much more helpful to contemplate what the irritation is trying to communicate to me.

And since doing this, I've found the decisions I make in response to an irritation are always significantly beneficial for my wellbeing and my income.

For example, over the past year I started to feel increasingly bothered about offering a free newsletter.

I did my best to ignore this feeling because it didn't seem logical not to have one; I mean everyone has a free newsletter, right?

And a freebie is the way to do it…or is it?

But then as I allowed myself to explore why I felt irritated, I uncovered what is true for me. What I really desired is to have a newsletter exclusively for clients and students.

I didn't know if this would be a good idea, but I went and removed the option on my website to join my newsletter list.

In its place I wrote "Looking for my newsletter sign-up? When you enrol in one of my tiny courses, live classes, or mentorships you'll have the option to receive occasional updates and event invitations from me."

The moment I published this change, I felt so incredibly good!

And, what happened next was equally incredible.

The following month my course sales doubled, and sales have continued at this level or higher since then.

My removing of the subscribe option caused people to go ahead and purchase what they needed.

Now, I am not suggesting you should go and do as I have done.

What I am encouraging you to do is look for the wisdom in irritation in your business.

Here are some questions to ask next time you notice a niggling irritation arise:

- What is this irritation trying to tell me?

- What change might I need to make in my business systems or how I offer my gifts?

The answers might surprise you!

❯❯❯ 12 ❮❮❮

Cause people to pause

Most marketing strategies are designed to make signing up, registering, and enrolling a no-brainer for our ideal customers. The name of the game is to do whatever it takes to push people over the edge to 'sign up now!'

Initially, I followed along with these practices, but then my conscience caught up with me.

It felt wrong to tantalise people (through discounting and the like) into signing up for things that they don't need, or don't have room on their plate for.

The thought of my creations gathering dust on people's computers also bothered me.

So, my mantra became "I want to make it a brainer."

What this means is that I want people to pause and think twice before they sign up for anything I offer. I want them to consider if they really need it, and if they really have space for it.

Here's how I go about doing this:

- I rarely offer discounts, and when I do, it's usually to existing clients and students.

- When there was an option to join my email list, instead of asking for the bare minimum (name and email address), I asked a couple of questions that required responses. Those who found this to be too much to ask moved on; those who really wanted to hear from me answered them.

- I don't offer money-back guarantees. I found this encourages people to act too quickly, skim over the details of the offering, and not fully consider what they are committing to.

- Apart from my publicly available, ungated content, I don't currently offer anything for free.

- I'm also mindful of not pricing things too cheaply, because in addition to avoiding a sign-up being a no-brainer, I also want each offering to stand on its own merits.

Do you feel you would also like to cause people to pause? And if so, how could you go about that? Take a moment now to jot down any ideas.

>>> 13 <<<

Write marketing copy without sounding salesy

We're not taught to write in a way that reflects real human conversation, which is why so many people struggle with writing copy for their business.

Something that helped me years ago when I was still in my corporate job was reading 'Write Language' by Allan Pease and Paul Dunn.

My key takeaway from this book was to write in the same way as I speak. Sounds so incredibly simple, but it was a huge game changer for me.

I remember receiving this feedback from my CEO a little while after: "Dani, when I read your emails it's like you are right there with me in the room, I can hear your voice and everything."

The simplest path to writing in a more meaningful way that connects with your audience's heart and mind is to imagine you are talking to a friend.

Now think about it, you wouldn't open a conversation with that friend by asking several questions designed to make them feel inadequate, or to feel any pain they are experiencing more deeply.

And at the same time, you wouldn't ignore how they were feeling; you'd find a way to acknowledge that in some way because you know how important it is for your friend to feel seen and heard.

Here's how to take this simple human approach and apply it to how you write for your business:

1. Write and speak to your audience the way you would speak to a real human who was sitting next to you. How would that conversation go? Let the words flow and don't get caught up on what you think you 'should' say from a sales or marketing perspective.

2. Be generous. Share what you can to help them right now, even if they are not a paying client or on your email list.

If what you share helps them see things differently and take the next step towards resolving their challenge, then power to them, and you! This is part of your contribution to the world.

What you want to be creating through your copy is 'goodwill'.

And through this goodwill you will be the one your readers turn to when they are ready to receive support with their challenges and goals.

Pause for a moment and see if there is a piece of content that comes to mind (e.g. a blog, email automation, sales page) that is calling out for a revision.

If so, make a note of that before reading on.

⫸ 14 ⫷

Make your creations digestible

When something is digestible, it means there is an ease by which it can be taken in, assimilated, understood, completed, and implemented.

And this is what we want for our readers, watchers, students, and clients, don't we?

We want them to walk away from engaging with our content feeling inspired, rather than overloaded with information.

More is not better, and people are really wising up to this.

They are seeking simplicity and smaller chunks of information that they can act upon straight away, and they are willing to pay more to receive it.

This is why my tiny courses have been so popular.

Tiny courses typically consist of 5-7 concise lessons that can be consumed within about one hour, rather than several hours, as is the case for most courses.

Digestibility is always a top priority when I am creating blogs, videos, newsletters, and any kind of educational content.

But digestibility is more than just the amount of content, it's also about how pleasing and easy it is for the eyes.

Use the following checklist to assess the digestibility of your creations.

Digestibility checklist:

- It doesn't look or sound like an Ad.

- Your personal experience and point of view are threaded throughout your creation.

- Your feature image (if there is one) describes what your intended reader/watcher wants, rather than their current pain.

- The headline or opening sentence speaks to something the reader is experiencing, interested in, or concerned about.

- Paragraphs are short and therefore easy to read.

- There are not too many ideas trying to be presented at once.

- Website text size is large enough and dark enough to be read with ease. (Medium.com is a good site to compare your website text with.)

- There is minimal use of UPPERCASE and emojis (which are often distracting to the eye).

Before reading on, make a note of any content or training presentations you want to revise so they are more digestible.

15

Market your message more than your offers

Tad Hargrave of Marketing for Hippies coined the term 'market your message' and the phrase perfectly captures the essence of how we can approach marketing in a meaningful and holistic way.

Your message is a melting pot of your knowledge, experience, point of view, and values, combined with specific challenges and goals people have.

When you think about your favourite brands, personalities, or coaches, you will no doubt find that you favour them due to the messages they transmit.

The entire process of marketing is transformed and feels good when we shift our attention to our message, rather than promoting our offerings at every turn.

For example, I receive way more interest in my offers when I share my personal perspective and experiences, as opposed to when I promote my offers directly.

You might be thinking, "Yes okay, but what is my message?"

Firstly, I think of my own message as being made up of several sub-messages.

These sub-messages have emerged over time through my lived experience and come together to create a certain feeling or vibe around my work.

Let's look at one of my messages, 'growing by slowing', and reverse engineer how it came about:

This message surfaced from my journey of being a high achiever and always pushing forward, striving for quick success and setting big money goals (that kept not being achieved).

I was able to accomplish great things by hustling, but the energy required was enormous and the results were not long lasting. As a result, I ended up very tired and wired.

What I desired most was sustainable success.

Success that wound not cost me my wellbeing.

Then one morning during some quiet reflection, I received some unexpected guidance.

I was sitting on my bed in a lotus position, eyes closed, and had just asked myself a question about how I could experience more joy and ease in my business.

Immediately I heard the words 'Aim lower'.

My eyes shot open.

I could not believe what I'd just heard.

The words were in my own voice, but not something I would ever think (or desire) to say.

After sitting there for a few minutes in disbelief, wondering what just happened, I then found myself wondering what it would look like for me to aim lower.

As I contemplated this, I started to experience what I can only describe as a pool of joy rising up from my base and flooding my belly.

I immediately took this as a visceral confirmation of the message I had just received.

For the next few months, I experimented with lowering my goals and slowing my pace, which felt so good and calmed my nervous system.

And then the magic happened!

I made more progress in these few months than I had made in the past few years, and my business finally got the lift-off I'd always wanted.

When I started sharing about this epiphany of aiming lower and slower, and the effect it had on my business, it stopped people in their tracks.

This message really spoke to their heart and soul, and made them want to hear more from me.

Here is what we can learn from this example:

1. That our messages are birthed from our own personal journeys and breakthroughs.

2. Messages are not plucked from the air based on what we think people want to hear, nor do they need to be based on a gap in the marketplace that we could fill.

Drawing out your message can be challenging, especially if you are doing it on your own.

If you feel you'd benefit from guidance in this area, I recommend taking my tiny course 'Organise Your Message'. OYM is a step-by-step system for translating your knowledge, point of view, values, and audience needs, into marketing content and sales pages.

⟫⟫⟫ 16 ⟪⟪⟪

Become discoverable

To really appreciate what 'discoverability' means for your business, first we need to talk about visibility.

Visibility is a pro-active, engagement and energy intensive approach to marketing.

Visibility typically requires a presence on social media and showing up regularly in newsfeeds, online communities, Stories, Reels, and Lives.

And therein lies the problem.

Most of the highly sensitive people I speak with don't want to 'have to' be on social media all the time, or they want to step away from it altogether.

What they do want is to have some means for people to know they exist that do not rely on one-on-one conversations or social media engagement.

This is where discoverability comes in.

Discoverability is a more laid-back, passive approach to marketing whereby our ideal audience is able to discover our work when they are intentionally searching for solutions that they need right now.

For example, 80% of my students and clients find me through Google and YouTube searches.

These are not searches for my name or generic terms such as 'business coach' — they are searches for specific topics that I speak about in my publicly available content.

When I first started to become discoverable (i.e. receiving an increase in organic visitors to my website), I had not done any intentional search engine optimization (SEO).

I simply shared helpful insights from my own experiences, and people happened to be searching for this same information.

In addition, I named these pieces of content in a very practical way. I didn't try to be clever with my titles, I just aimed to have the benefit of reading or watching in the title.

How you can become more discoverable:

- Have easily accessible content in the public domain (e.g. blogs and YouTube videos) that people could potentially find when they are searching for information they need.

- When naming your blogs or videos, be very practical. Aim to have the benefit of reading or watching your content in the headline.

- Look back on the existing content and resources that you have created for clients and consider how you could repurpose those pieces into a blog or YouTube video.

The suggestions above are an easy starting point. If you'd like to focus more on being discoverable, then take a look at my tiny course 'Discoverability and Audience Building'.

Take a moment to note down any actions you feel inspired to take to become more discoverable.

>>> 17 <<<

Lean back and let
clients chase you

One of the first things we tend to learn about marketing is that we need to hustle, spend hours engaging, and chase after clients in order to have people buy from us.

And like me, you may have found these strategies depleting to your body, mind, and soul.

As I began questioning these widespread marketing norms, it dawned on me how much I detest feeling like I need to chase after clients — or anyone for that matter.

Marketing is very similar to dating.

When we feel someone is desperate for love and attention, we give them a wide berth.

Whereas when we see someone is relaxed, confident in their own skin, and not trying to impress us — we feel more drawn to them.

Here are some ways that I have created an environment where the right clients chase after me:

- Leaning back physically and mentally, rather than forward. For example, leaning back ever so slightly in my chair while working on my computer or in client sessions has shifted my energy and brought what I want towards me.

- Having publicly available content that people can easily access before they commit to doing anything with me, rather than locking my knowledge up inside email opt-ins and private communities.

- Being transparent about my pricing. I display my prices on my website because this puts people at ease, makes me approachable (to the right people), and alleviates the need for any awkward 'price reveal' moments later on.

- And my personal favourite, closing my eyes and imagining clients eagerly chasing after me.

These practices have also been excellent for my self care. Try them out for yourself; you'll see what I mean.

Final words

I hope these chapters have inspired you to think differently and sparked fresh hope and possibilities for you, your business, and your sense of wellbeing.

Please visit danigardner.com/book-resources for further information on the suggestions I've made in this book.

Quiet Marketing
Contemplations

Each of the following contemplations relates to a chapter of this book and acts as a summary of actions you can take:

1. What is your definition of success?

2. What can you do to minimise peer distraction and practice tunnel vision?

3. How can you reduce digital distraction?

4. What needs to change so you can give yourself more breathing space in business?

5. How will you remember to consider your Human Design 'strategy' when creating things in your business?

6. What 'output' are you prioritising right now?

7. How will you remember to 'play the whole tape through'?

8. Where are you making yourself more accessible than you really want to be?

9. What activities are you 'making' yourself do? If you were to be really 'you', how would you do things? What would you rather focus on?

10. What adjustments can you make so you can work from a smaller, more manageable plate?

11. Are there any irritations niggling away in the background? If so, what change might this irritation be calling you to make?

12. In what ways can you cause people to pause, so they make more conscious choices about where to invest their time and money?

13. Is there a blog or sales page that you feel needs revision, so it sounds more human and less salesy?

14. What content or training presentations could you revise so they feel more digestible?

15. How do you feel about threading more of your perspective/point of view throughout your content and marketing?

16. What action do you feel inspired to take to become more discoverable?

17. In what ways can you 'lean back' and allow clients to chase you?

Acknowledgements

First, I want to acknowledge my husband Jon for believing and investing in me from the very beginning of my entrepreneurial journey. I don't know where I would have ended up without your ever-present support.

Secondly, I am so grateful to have crossed paths with Alexandra Fransen and discovered the joy of all things tiny, including her tiny book course container, where this book was created.

Finally, I want to acknowledge the following people who have contributed to my entrepreneurial journey:

Andrea Hess

Amanda Jane Daley

Tad Hargrave

Gina De Vee

Tash Corbin

Melanie Midegs

Caroline Southwell

Natalie Kent

Christopher Power

Liz Melville

George Kao

Dr. Nathalie Martenik

Heather LaneMcCants

Delaney Van Baalen

Lucas Forstmeyer

About the Author

Danielle Gardner is a Business Mentor and author of *Quiet Marketing: A calm, minimal approach to business and online visibility for highly sensitive solopreneurs.*

She is known for having and teaching an unorthodox approach to business and marketing, one that people find to be a breath of fresh air and relaxing to their nervous system.

Danielle encourages coaches, healers and consultants to do things differently, question the so-called marketing rules, and to trust their ideas and preferences — especially when they contradict widespread business advice.

Find Danielle's latest articles,
online events and trainings at:
www.danigardner.com

CPSIA information can be obtained
at www.ICGtesting.com
Printed in the USA
BVHW051108081122
651446BV00005B/274

9 780645 313802